# Contents

Words in bold, **like this**, are explained in the Glossary.

# Hair, fur and feathers

Many animals have a covering of hair or feathers. People have hair. You can see the hair on people's heads, but most of their body hair is so fine, you cannot see it at all.

**Elizabeth Miles**

**www.heinemann.co.uk/library**
Visit our website to find out more information about **Heinemann Library** books.

To order:
☎ Phone 44 (0) 1865 888066
▤ Send a fax to 44 (0) 1865 314091
▢ Visit the Heinemann Bookshop at www.heinemann.co.uk/library to browse our
catalogue and order online.

First published in Great Britain by Heinemann Library, Halley Court, Jordan Hill, Oxford
OX2 8EJ, a division of Reed Educational and Professional Publishing Ltd. Heinemann is a registered trademark of Reed Educational &
Professional Publishing Limited.

OXFORD MELBOURNE AUCKLAND JOHANNESBURG BLANTYRE
GABORONE IBADAN PORTSMOUTH NH (USA) CHICAGO

Designed by David Oakley@Arnos Design
Originated by Dot Gradations
Printed in Hong Kong

ISBN 0 431 15326 4 (hardback)          ISBN 0 431 15332 9 (paperback)
06 05 04 03 02                          06 05 04 03
10 9 8 7 6 5 4 3 2 1                     10 9 8 7 6 5 4 3 2 1

**British Library Cataloguing in Publication Data**

Miles, Elizabeth
  Why do animals have fur and feathers
  1.Fur - Juvenile literature 2.Feathers - Juvenile
  literature 3.Physiology - Juvenile literature
  I.Title
  573.5'8'1

**Acknowledgements**
The Publishers would like to thank the following for permission to reproduce photographs: BBC Natural History Unit/Chris Packham
p. 24; BBC Natural History Unit/Jeff Foott pp. 13, 28; BBC Natural History Unit/Lynn M. Stone p. 15; BBC Natural History Unit/Neil
Bromhall p. 29; BBC Nautral History Unit/Staffan Widstrand p. 21; Bruce Coleman pp. 17, 26; Bruce Coleman/Kim Taylor p. 18; Corbis
p. 12; Digital Stock p. 30; digital vision p. 23; NHPA/Anthony Bannister p. 16; NHPA /Eric Soder p. 22; NHPA /Jany Sauvanet p. 20;
NHPA /Jeff Goodman p. 19; NHPA /John Shaw p. 27; NHPA /Kevin Shafer p. 25; NHPA /Martin Harvey p. 14.

Cover photograph reproduced with permission of Powerstock Zefa.

Our thanks to Claire Robinson, Head of Visitor Information and Education at London Zoo, for her help in the preparation of this book.

Every effort has been made to contact copyright holders of any material reproduced in this book. Any omissions will be rectified in
subsequent printings if notice is given to the Publisher.

Animal hair may be thin or thick, soft or rough. A coat of soft hair is often called fur. A sheep has a covering of wool. Wool is thick, curly hair.

# Fur for warmth

Coats of fur have two kinds of hair. The soft layer near the skin is called **underfur**. It keeps the animal warm. The outer layer of fur keeps the animal dry. A reindeer's fur keeps it warm and dry.

A polar bear lives in an icy-cold place. Its thick, furry coat helps to keep it warm. It can even walk on the cold ice because there is fur under its feet.

# Long fur and hair

Some animals have very long coats. The outer layer of a musk oxen's fur coat is made up of lots of very long hairs. Its long coat keeps it warm and dry in the cold and wind.

Golden lion tamarins have long coats of orange hair. They live in leafy tree-tops in forests. Their long, brightly coloured coats help them to see each other.

# Fur that changes colour

Many **mammals** grow thicker coats in winter and then **shed** them in summer. In winter, an Arctic fox has a thick, white coat of fur. It keeps the fox warm and helps the fox to hide in the snow.

When the snow melts in summer, the Arctic fox loses a lot of its white winter fur. It is left with a cooler, darker coat. This summer coat matches the brown earth.

# Shapes and patterns of hair

The shape and pattern of an animal's hair can be very important. It gives a message to other animals. A **male** lion has a **mane** to make it look fierce and strong.

A giraffe has dark patches on its body to help it to hide. It can hardly be seen in the shadows of a tree. Giraffes need to hide from **predators** such as lions.

# Sensitive hairs

As well as a covering of hairs, some animals have special, sensitive hairs. These hairs help the animal to feel the world around it. Wombats use their **whiskers** to feel their way around.

Many **insects** have what look like hairs. They are really special **scales**. A moth uses them to taste with its feet! The tiny, sensitive 'hairs' on its feet help the moth to know what it is standing on.

# Hairs like spikes

Some animals have hard, sharp hair. A porcupine has a covering of quills, or very prickly hairs. If an animal attacks, the porcupine sticks up its quills and runs backwards to prick its enemy.

A hedgehog has a covering of spines. These are strong, stiff hairs with sharp tips. If it is attacked, the hedgehog rolls up into a spiny ball.

# Feathers

Birds have a covering of feathers instead of hair. A snowy owl lives in cold snow and ice. Even its feet and beak are covered in feathers for warmth.

Baby birds like these ducklings could easily get cold, but they have lots of soft, fluffy feathers to keep them warm. These soft feathers are called down.

# Feathers for flight

A bird needs feathers to fly. Its wings have long, flat, stiff feathers. Each feather has many tiny strands, joined to a hollow **shaft** that runs down the middle.

shaft

Birds use their feathers to fly far and high. The feathers make the wings wide and flat, and light but strong. Birds either flap their wings, or **soar** through the air like this condor.

# Waterproof feathers

Many birds have oily **waterproof** feathers that do not soak up water. A pelican has waterproof feathers. It can dive underwater to catch fish and come up dry.

Birds that swim underwater need to stay warm. A penguin swims in icy-cold sea water. A layer of closely packed feathers keeps its body warm and dry.

# Plain or colourful feathers

Different birds have different coloured feathers. A nightjar has feathers that match where it lives. It can sit on its nest without being seen by a **predator**.

Some birds have very colourful feathers.
**Male** quetzals have beautiful, colourful
feathers. They show them off to **female** birds.

# Cleaning hair or feathers

Animals take care of their hair or feathers to keep their coats clean and healthy. Cheetahs lick their fur to keep it clean. A cheetah also licks its **cub's** fur.

Birds **preen** their feathers to keep them clean and tidy for flying. They use their beak to make sure their feathers are **waterproof** and to get rid of any dirt.

# No fur

Some **mammals** do not have hair or fur, but they need to keep warm. A whale has a layer of fat under its thick skin to keep it warm. The fat is called blubber.

A naked mole rat is called that because it has hardly any hair. It lives in warm places and stays underground. It does not need thick hair to keep warm.

# Fact file

● Elephants and rhinoceroses have very little hair because they have thick skin and live in warm places.

● Some **mammals** make themselves look bigger by fluffing out their fur. Cats do this to frighten off other cats.

● Birds have different numbers of feathers. They may have as few as 940 or as many as 25,000!

Cheetahs can run faster than any other animal.

# Glossary

**cubs**  young animals, such as cheetahs or lions

**female**  if a female is a parent it is the mother

**insects**  small animals with six legs and three parts to their body

**male**  if a male is a parent it is the father

**mammals**  animals that feed their babies with the mother's milk. People are mammals.

**mane**  long thick hair on the neck of animals such as lions or horses

**predators**  animals that hunt other animals for food

**preen**  how a bird keeps its feathers clean and tidy with its beak

**scales**  thin, flat pieces that cover animals such as fish and snakes

**shaft**  long, narrow part that runs down the centre of a feather

**shed**  when an animal sheds its coat, hairs drop off

**soar**  when a bird flies high without flapping its wings

**underfur**  layer of soft fur near the skin

**waterproof**  protected from getting wet

**whiskers**  hairs near the mouth and nose of an animal, such as a cat. These hairs help the animal to feel the world around it.

# Index

# FUR and FEATHERS

Have you ever wondered why some animals have a tail, or scales, or a huge nose? And do you know why some animals have eyes on stalks, or ears they can swivel, or a sticky tongue? Read the **Why Do Animals Have** books to find the answers and lots more besides.

This series reveals the incredible diversity of the external parts of animals. It also looks at why they are so different, exploring how animals have adapted to their environment, and how we can group living things according to similarities and differences that we can observe.

Each book includes:
• stunning photos with simple, clear text
• fact file
• glossary, more books to read and index.

**Titles in the series:**

These titles are also available in hardback.

ISBN 0-431-15332-9

9 780431 153322

**Heinemann**
**LIBRARY**

Find out about the full range of Heinemann Library resources at
www.heineman...

# NOSES

Heinemann
firSt
Library

# WHY DO ANIMALS HAVE

# NOSES

**Elizabeth Miles**

**www.heinemann.co.uk/library**
Visit our website to find out more information about **Heinemann Library** books.

To order:
 Phone 44 (0) 1865 888066
 Send a fax to 44 (0) 1865 314091
💻 Visit the Heinemann Bookshop at www.heinemann.co.uk/library to browse our catalogue and order online.

First published in Great Britain by Heinemann Library, Halley Court, Jordan Hill, Oxford OX2 8EJ, a division of Reed Educational and Professional Publishing Ltd. Heinemann is a registered trademark of Reed Educational & Professional Publishing Limited.

OXFORD  MELBOURNE  AUCKLAND  JOHANNESBURG  BLANTYRE
GABORONE  IBADAN  PORTSMOUTH NH (USA)  CHICAGO

Designed by David Oakley@Arnos Design
Originated by Dot Gradations
Printed in Hong Kong

J573.26
1406040

ISBN 0 431 15312 4 (hardback)
06 05 04 03 02
10 9 8 7 6 5 4 3 2 1

ISBN 0 431 15318 3 (paperback)
06 05 04 03
10 9 8 7 6 5 4 3 2 1

**British Library Cataloguing in Publication Data**

Miles, Elizabeth
  Why do animals have noses
  1.Nose - Juvenile literature 2.Physiology - Juvenile literature
  I.Title
  573.2'6

**Acknowledgements**
The Publishers would like to thank the following for permission to reproduce photographs: BBC Natural History Unit/Bruce Davidson p. 12; BBC Natural History Unit/Jeff Foott pp. 20, 22; BBC Natural History Unit/Lawrence A. Michael p. 7; Bruce Coleman Collection pp. 9, 16; Bruce Coleman Collection/Jane Burton p. 23; Bruce Coleman Collection/Staffan Widstrand p. 6; Bruce Coleman Collection/Gunter Ziesler pp. 13, 27; Corbis p. 17; Corbis/Owen Franklen p. 15; digital vision pp. 10, 30; Gareth Boden p. 4; NHPA p. 26; NHPA/Andy Rouse p. 14; NHPA/Anthony Bannister p. 8; NHPA/Kevin Schafer p.5; Oxford Scientific Films/Bates Littlehales p. 29; Oxford Scientific Films/Ben Osborne p. 21; Oxford Scientific Films/Mark Hamblin p. 25; Oxford Scientific Films/Michael Habicat p. 24; Oxford Scientific Films/David Fox p. 28; Photodisc pp. 5, 18, 19; Science Photo Library/Mauro Fermariello p. 11.

Cover photograph reproduced with permission of Photodisc.

Our thanks to Claire Robinson, Head of Visitor Information and Education at London Zoo, for her help in the preparation of this book.

Every effort has been made to contact copyright holders of any material reproduced in this book. Any omissions will be rectified in subsequent printings if notice is given to the Publisher.